Spiritual Warfare

Spiritual Warfare

Volume I

Howard Grant

Spiritual Warfare Volume I
ISBN: 978-0-88144-252-6
Copyright © 2010 by Howard Grant

Published by
Thorncrown Publishing
9731 East 54th Street
Tulsa, OK 74146
www.thorncrownpublishing.com

Table of Contents

Acknowledgement

I want to express my deepest gratitude to all those who have assisted me in putting this book together. To some people putting something so small together is no big deal, but to me it was grand. So "thank you" to Karen DePass—my sister in Christ, Shari-Ann Grant—my daughter, and my wife, Sharon Grant. I am also grateful to the rest of my family for their cooperation. It is my prayer that the Almighty God will reward them greatly and grant them His peace. Above all, I want to thank the Almighty God, through His son Jesus Christ, for the occasion of a mission trip in which my daughter was involved. It was my daughter's experience that inspired me to write this book. God be praised.

Howard H. Grant, Sr.

Foreword

As the born-again children of God, we must be aware of the fact that as long as we are His (God's) people, we are subject to hatred and attacks from His enemy. Jesus Christ gave us the heads-up before He left; He said that if they hated Him, they would hate you as well. In John 15:18-19 it reads, "If the world hate you, ye know that it hated me before *it hated* you. If ye were of the world, the world would love his own: but because ye are not of the world, but I have chosen you out of the world, therefore the world hateth you."

According to the Word of God, the princes of this world brought about the cruel and brutal crucifixion of Jesus Christ. This they did because of their chronic hatred of God and everything godly. Who are these princes? Clearly, they are not mere human beings of flesh and blood. Ephesians 6:12—a scripture we will examine at length—says, "For we wrestle not against flesh and blood, but against principalities, against powers, against the rulers of the darkness of this world, against spiritual wickedness in high places." There are powerful, demonic beings in the heavens that exert their influence on the population of earth, with a distinct hatred for God's people. The Word of God makes it clear that we, His children, are wrestling with spiritual forces. We are in a state of war, and there are weapons at our disposal that are absolutely effective against our enemies.

Our Father wants us to be mentally and spiritually aware at all times, because large parts of our battles are fought in the mental and spiritual realm. 2 Corinthians 10:3-5 emphasizes the mental aspect of our battle. Verse 5 says we must constantly be "Cast[ing] down imaginations, and every high thing that exalteth itself against the knowledge of God, and bringing into captivity every thought to the obedience of Christ." It is the will of God that we consciously control all aspects of our thought life. There are three words mentioned in the above scripture that must not be overlooked— IMAGINATION, KNOWLEDGE, and THOUGHT. All three are found between our ears as functions of the mind. Make no mistake about it—the mind is the primary battlefield in which we fight. So many people seem to be unaware, but many spiritual battles are won when we are determined to apply the Word of God in all our experiences, despite the temptation to do otherwise and satisfy our pleasures. We must arm ourselves with the knowledge of the Word of God and win our battles for the kingdom.

You will notice that in this book the biblical quotes are from several different versions of the Bible. The King James Version happens to be the most common. However, I like the way some of the other versions present part of the scriptures (such as the New King James Version, New Living Translation, and New International Version). With that being said, you do not have to read all the different versions presented as you read this book. Any particular version of your choice will essentially give you the same message.

In an effort to provide greater clarity in understanding this book, I thought that some definitions should be provided. Below are some definitions for some keywords from one of the foundational scriptures used in establishing, supporting, and clarifying the subject of spiritual war[1].

Principalities: 1) a state ruled by a prince; 2) the position or authority of a prince or chief ruler.

Power: ability to do or act; a person or thing that possesses or exercises authority or influence; a deity; divinity.

Dark: wickedness or evil; Satan, the prince of darkness.

Wickedness: evil or morally bad; in principle sinful iniquitous.

Be blessed.

---

[1] Provided by dictionary.com

A Simple and Divine Message

The Word of God is full of divine wisdom and revelation, but it is so often overlooked because of the simplicity of its presentation. "Love thy neighbor as thyself" would make a perfect world. There would be no crime against humanity, no war, and everyone would live in perfect peace. There would be no need for guards, soldiers, or police. There would be worldwide harmony. It is mind-boggling when you think about how different things would be if everyone were to live by this little command spoken by perfection Himself. God's word is perfect; He speaks with ultimate wisdom that cannot be improved upon, regardless of how simple it may appear to be. Let us open our ears to the wisdom of God. It is calling out to us, and it is always rich and potent. The book of Proverbs says that wisdom cries in the street in some of the most common or visible places in the city, calling to the simple. Proverbs 1:20-23 (New Living Translation) says this:

20 Wisdom shouts in the streets. She cries out in the public square.

21 She calls out to the crowds along the main street, and to those in front of city hall.

22 *"You simpletons!" she cries. "How long will you go on being sim-pleminded? How long will you mockers relish your mocking? How long will you fools fight the facts?*

23 *Come here and listen to me! I'll pour out the spirit of wisdom upon you and make you wise".*

It is incredible to see how deep the simple truth can be when the light of revelation and understanding is turned on in our hearts and minds. Understanding has many levels. Sometimes truth is so deep it seems unfathomable. Even so, revelation of the Word of God begins at the surface, long before we begin our descent into its depth. Such is the nature of the Word of God. We should not be surprised, for God and His Word are one, "In the beginning was the word, and the word was with God, and the word was God," John 1:1 (KJV). He is infinite, and so is His Word.

The Ultimate Professor

The sovereign God is our master teacher. He prepares for his classes hundreds and thousands of years before they come into existence. He employs theoretical, practical, and spiritual means to infuse us with His truth. The practical is often of a historical nature, but very powerful in the way it demonstrates and illustrates the theoretical lessons we are learning today in the New Testament. "For whatsoever things were written aforetime were written for our learning, that we through patience and comfort of the Scriptures might have hope," Romans 15:4 (KJV).

The New Testament is loaded with theoretical lessons, one of which we are looking at today. The subject is spiritual warfare, and the scriptures we are looking at are: 2 Corinthians 10:3-5, Ephesians 6:10-18, Daniel 10:1-20, and Ezekiel 28:1-20. We have already looked at the fact that although we are living in the realm of the natural (the physical), we don't war in the natural, and the weapons that we war with are not natural, physical weapons. We are also made aware that our fights, for the most part, take place first and foremost in our minds and in the realm of the spirit. The enemies are powerful and wicked spirits that rule over different areas of the earth. They exert their influence upon the rulers as well as the common people in general.

Strongholds

The enemy has managed to set up strongholds in so many Christians as well as in those of us that do not know God. In the areas of enemy strongholds, principalities and powers have the upper hand. Our victory begins with awareness and knowledge of the Word of God. Ephesians 6:12 (KJV) says,

> For we wrestle not against flesh and blood, but against principalities, against powers, against the rulers of the darkness of this world, against spiritual wickedness in high places.

Our spiritual wars are against principalities and powers in high places. Their greatest effort is to influence our mind, because our minds interface with the realm of the spirit. The fact is we don't see demonic spirits running around with guns, knives, or explosives. We don't see them fighting and killing people; we don't see them fighting wars. To accomplish whatever they want to, they employ human beings by influencing our minds. It is in the mind that we wrestle, and there is no victory without the Word.

Ephesians 6:13-18 (KJV) says,

13 Wherefore take unto you the whole armour of God, that ye may be able to withstand in the evil day, and having done all, to stand.

14 Stand therefore, having your loins girt about with truth, and having on the breastplate of righteousness;

15 And your feet shod with the preparation of the gospel of peace;

16 Above all, taking the shield of faith, wherewith ye shall be able to quench all the fiery darts of the wicked.

17 And take the helmet of salvation, and the sword of the Spirit, which is the word of God:

18 Praying always with all prayer and supplication in the Spirit, and watching thereunto with all perseverance and supplication for all saints.

For emphasis and clarity, let us take a look at what a stronghold is according to 2 Corinthians 10:3-4, with special emphasis on verse 4. Afterward we will look at a practical battle in the book of Daniel demonstrating the New Testament theories/scriptures that we have read. In the New Living Translation it reads:

We are human, but we don't wage war as humans do. We use God's mighty weapons, not worldly weapons, to knock down the strongholds of human reasoning and to destroy false arguments.

Where Are These Strongholds?

Where are these strongholds located? The scripture makes it clear for us—they are in our minds. From the scripture, it is obvious that our weapons are spiritual, but our walk is not. Our walk is the way we live our lives. Our walk shows in our attitude, mannerisms, and behavior, which are controlled by our minds. Every word that we speak and every action that we take first originates in the mind, which is under our control. 2 Corinthians chapter 10:4-5 speaks of casting down <u>imaginations</u>, things that exalt themselves above our <u>knowledge of God</u>, and about bringing every <u>thought into captivity</u>.

Our knowledge, our thoughts, and our imagination are all in our minds, and this is where all our battles are fought. In the battlefield of the mind, there are areas of our thought life where deception, ignorance, or negative habits prevail, and we, for the most part, unknowingly embrace these spiritually erroneous thoughts and beliefs that are consistent with the enemy of our souls. Through our ignorance, or his deception, the enemy fortifies himself in our thoughts and thus in our lives. By deception, we cooperate with the enemy and protect his interest in our lives. This leads to our own demise. There is a reason he is called a deceiver, because he can have us embracing, defending, and protecting a lie; thinking it is truth, and it is our own mind.

I once saw a documentary on TV about a little bird that can reproduce without making a nest or sitting on its own eggs. It simply waits for a particular bird of similar size to make its nest and lay its eggs. At some point in time, when the nest is unguarded, the lazy bird goes into its neighbor's nest and pushes out the eggs that have been laid there. It then lays its own eggs in the neighbor's nest and flies away. When the neighbor returns to its nest, it does not realize that there are new eggs in there or that the eggs belong to another bird. It simply sits on the eggs of a stranger, feeds them, and guards them until they are grown and old enough to be independent, without a clue that they reared the chicks of a stranger. This is a classic example of what the enemy does to many of us when we are distracted. In our case, our thought lives have been invaded, and we have no clue; we simply guard non-biblical concepts, beliefs, and ideas thinking that they are truth, but they are the enemy's lies.

When Our Thoughts Exalt Themselves Above Our Knowledge of Christ

The enemy's stronghold in our thought life gives him great advantages, which have a negative impact on our lives. Let us say, for example, our thoughts or imagination lead us to believe that pride is sometimes justifiable, despite what God has to say about pride. This would not be uncommon in our time. Many believe that if you are really good at what you do, it is okay to show-off, boast, or beat your chest a little bit about your ability. This boasting is born out of thoughts that are allowed to exalt themselves above the knowledge of God. God's Word encourages humility, and the enemy encourages pride. In this case the failure in being humble, would be allowing the thought of pride to determine our actions; on the other hand, when humility triumphs over pride, pride is held captive to humility. Humility in our actions is what God requires, and it is spiritual victory over pride. Let's look at some scriptures on the benefits of humility.

And whosoever shall exalt himself shall be abased; and he that shall humble himself shall be exalted.

Matthew 23:12 (KJV)

Whosoever therefore shall humble himself as this little child, the same is greatest in the kingdom of heaven.

Matthew 18:4 (KJV)

Those who walk in pride, as a result, will experience the consequences of pride, the end of which is destruction. In Proverbs 16:18 of the New Living Translation, we see a little of what the Word has to say about pride.

Pride goes before destruction,
and haughtiness before a fall.

And in Proverbs 16:5 of the same version, which reads:

The Lord detests the proud; they will surely be punished.

People Hurt by Their Own Pride

L et us take a look at the negative impact of pride on the lives of a few Bible characters.

King Herod

King Herod's story is a reminder to us that all our abilities come from God. There is nothing we possess that was not given to us, so before we beat our chests about our achievements, we must remember the source of our abilities with gratitude. Believe it or not, to do otherwise is to embrace pride, which puts us on a collision course with our Maker. The result is a no-brainer. God resists the proud, and He is the only one that is omnipotent, omniscient, and omnipresent. Herod learned this the hard way.

> 21 And upon a set day Herod, arrayed in royal apparel, sat upon his throne, and made an oration unto them.

> 22 And the people gave a shout, saying, "It is the voice of a god, and not of a man."

23 And immediately the angel of the Lord smote him, because he gave not God the glory: and he was eaten of worms, and gave up the ghost.

Acts 12:21-23 (KJV)

King Nebuchadnezzar

The second example is King Nebuchadnezzar in the book of Daniel. This king was so full of himself that, despite the fact that his fate was foretold in a dream, in Daniel 4:27 (NIV), he could not help himself. *"Therefore, O king, be pleased to accept my advice: renounce your sins by doing what is right, and your wickedness by being kind to the oppressed. It may be that then your prosperity will continue."* He was encouraged to make the necessary changes to avoid his fate, but he clearly did not.

Months after he was told about what would come, he walked into his palace and began to boast about his personal accomplishments in all his pomp and pride. His action fulfilled his dream, and his pride brought him very low. Daniel 4:29-33 (NIV):

29 Twelve months later, as the king was walking on the roof of the royal palace of Babylon, 30 he said, "Is not this the great Babylon I have built as the royal residence, by my mighty power and for the glory of my majesty?"

31 The words were still on his lips when a voice came from heaven, "This is what is decreed for you, King Nebuchadnezzar: Your royal authority has been taken from you. 32 You will be driven away from people and will live with the wild animals; you will eat grass like cattle. Seven times will pass by for you until you acknowledge that the Most High is sovereign over the kingdoms of men and gives them to anyone he wishes."

33 Immediately what had been said about Nebuchadnezzar was fulfilled. He was driven away from people and ate grass like cattle. His body was drenched with the dew of heaven until his hair grew like the feathers of an eagle and his nails like the claws of a bird.

King David

King David lost a spiritual battle when the devil convinced him to number Israel. Despite the fact that Jo'ab discouraged him from doing so, he did it anyway. We see this in 1 Chronicles 21:2-5 (KJV).

> *2 And David said to Jo'ab and to the rulers of the people, "Go, number Israel from Beer-sheba even to Dan; and bring the number of them to me, that I may know it."*
>
> *3 And Jo'ab answered, "The LORD make his people a hundred times so many more as they be: but, my lord the king, are they not all my lord's servants? Why then doth my lord require this thing? Why will he be a cause of trespass to Israel?"*
>
> *4 Nevertheless the king's word prevailed against Jo'ab. Wherefore Jo'ab departed, and went throughout all Israel, and came to Jerusalem.*
>
> *5 And Jo'ab gave the sum of the number of the people unto David. And all they of Israel were a thousand and a hundred thousand men that drew sword: and Judah was four hundred threescore and ten thousand men that drew sword.*

The blessing of God was upon King David, and he was winning his battles against all his enemies. When David numbered Israel, he was attributing his God-given victories to the size of his army; taking pride in the size of his army rather than God Himself who gave the victory. This was very displeasing to God. His pride brought judgment upon both him and Israel, and, as a result, 70,000 died. Let's take a look at 1 Chronicles 21:7-14 (KJV).

> *7 And God was displeased with this thing; therefore He smote Israel.*
>
> *8 And David said unto God, "I have sinned greatly, because I have done this thing: but now, I beseech thee, do away the iniquity of thy servant; for I have done very foolishly."*

9 And the LORD spoke unto Gad, David's seer, saying,

10 "Go and tell David, saying,' Thus saith the LORD, I offer thee three things: choose thee one of them, that I may do it unto thee."

11 So Gad came to David, and said unto him, "Thus saith the LORD, Choose thee

12 Either three years' famine; or three months to be destroyed before thy foes, while that the sword of thine enemies overtaketh thee; or else three days the sword of the LORD, even the pestilence, in the land, and the angel of the LORD destroying throughout all the coasts of Israel. Now therefore advise thyself what word I shall bring again to him that sent me."

13 And David said unto Gad, "I am in a great strait: let me fall now into the hand of the LORD; for very great are His mercies: but let me not fall into the hand of man."

14 So the LORD sent pestilence upon Israel: <u>and there fell of Israel seventy thousand men.</u>

As a side note, having read the above scripture we should be made aware that the pride of a leader could affect those he leads. Keep your leader in prayer.

The Enemy

Of all the angels that God created, there was none more exalted, beautiful and powerful than Lucifer the cherub, and there is none that has been brought lower than he as a result of pride. Let's take a look at the New King James Version of Isaiah 14:11-15.

11 Thy pomp is brought down to the grave, and the noise of thy viols: the worm is spread under thee, and the worms cover thee.

12 How art thou fallen from heaven, O Lucifer, son of the morning! How art thou cut down to the ground, which didst weaken the nations!

13 For thou hast said in thine heart, "I will ascend into heaven, I will exalt my throne above the stars of God, I will sit also upon the mount of the congregation, in the sides of the north;

14 I will ascend above the heights of the clouds; I will be like the most High."

15 Yet thou shalt be brought down to Sheol, to the uttermost parts of the pit.

We cannot forget our weapons. They are embodied in the Word of God. A few examples of these are prayer, fasting, worship, praise, faith, and obedience. Chapters 11 and 12 of Hebrews are great sources. These are but a few. In a later chapter, we will take an in-depth look at these and how they are demonstrated in the Old Testament scriptures. We cannot take our focus off the Word. It is the only way to avoid strongholds. If we lose sight of the Word or modify it in any way, we will be walking in darkness. It is for this reason the Bible says, "thy word is a lamp unto my feet and a light unto my path." Without the Word, our walk will be in darkness.

The Purpose of Strongholds

What is the purpose of these strongholds in our lives? They are to fulfill the purpose and objectives of the enemy. His ultimate objective is to steal, kill, and destroy. He is exalted in strongholds and has greater impact on our lives. We must never forget to cast down imaginations and thoughts that do not measure up to the Word. For example, thoughts that involve anger, lust, lies, pride, etc. We must be vigilant against thoughts that exalt themselves against what we know about the Word of God, thoughts that seek to justify doing the opposite of what we know the Word requires of us. We must capture them so that the Word of God alone will determine our action. We must always be mindful of the Word of God.

For though we live in the world, we do not wage war as the world does.

4 The weapons we fight with are not weapons of the world. On the contrary, they have divine power to demolish strongholds.

5 We demolish arguments and every pretention that sets itself up against the knowledge of God, and we take captive every thought to make it obedient to Christ.

2 Corinthians 10:3-5 (NIV)

Daniel's Practical Spiritual Battle

I n a practical sense, we see Daniel in a war in which he triggered a spiritual confrontation in the heavens over Persia. It happened on his knees, in prayer and fasting, where he spoke to the Almighty God, who responded by sending one of his mighty angels to Daniel with an answer to his prayer. It is comforting to know that nothing could stop God from hearing Daniel's prayer. He was heard on the first day, so will you and I be, when we call upon our God in fasting and prayer. We know from reading the book of Daniel that the angels of God cannot lose when they fight on our behalf, because the ALMIGHTY GOD is behind them, and He cannot be a loser. He created power, and He is the personification of power. He is the ultimate source in heaven above and on the earth beneath. The Word says He is omnipotent; whatever power anyone possesses originally came from God. The time is coming when all demonic powers will be destroyed, including the chief of all demons, the devil, who is no match for the great power of God. Before we go on, let us look at a few examples of the power of God over the devil.

> *By the multitude of thy merchandise they have filled the midst of thee with violence, and thou has sinned: therefore I will cast thee*

as profane out of the mountain of God: and I will destroy thee, O covering cherub, from the midst of the stones of fire.

Ezekiel 28:16 (KJV)

And there was war in heaven. Michael and his angels fought against the dragon, and the dragon and his angels fought back,

8 but he was not strong enough, and they lost their place in heaven.

9 The great dragon was hurled down, that ancient serpent called the devil or Satan, who lead the whole earth astray. He was hurled to the earth, and his angels with him.

Revelation 12:7-9(NIV)

And I saw an angel coming down out of heaven, having the key of the abyss and holding in his hand a great chain.

2 He seized the dragon, that ancient serpent who is the devil, or Satan, and bound him for a thousand years.

3 He throw him into the abyss, and locked and sealed it over him, to keep him from deceiving the nations anymore until the thousand years were ended after that he must be set free for a short time.

Revelation 20:1-3 (NIV)

We Are Not at the Enemy's Mercy

We need not worry about what the devil can or cannot do to us when we are under God's covering or walking in His Word. The devil can't just do whatever he feels. In the book of Job, he could not touch Job without permission; however, from what we see in the scriptures, he has the freedom to tempt us, and not even Jesus Christ was immune. But if we yield our will to him, he can literally destroy individuals, families, even nations. Craftiness, trickery, and subtle deception are some of the ways he influences our thoughts and imagination. Our feelings, our emotions, and impressions on our hearts is where his primary work is done in our lives. Conflict with family and friends, as well as the desire to do wrong things, is all the work of the enemy. If we are not aware of this, it will be over before it begins.

We are prone to evil (Exodus 32:22), and according to Psalms 51:5, we were conceived in sin and shaped in iniquity. Our nature is defiled because of Adam, so sinful thoughts and desires will come to our hearts and minds, and we are tempted to embrace them. If we do, out of these minute temptations the enemy will create monsters. All of this is happening in our mind, and we, unable to see where the transition from the small to the great takes place, embrace the monster by yielding to temptation. The enemy knows how to exploit these small desires and transform them into giants. Imagine a radio receiving an inaudible signal, and someone turns the volume up so high that it shakes the room: this is how the enemy works with little thoughts, impressions, and desires. These thoughts may have been born out of our sinful nature, but when the enemy attaches himself, it then gets to the point where we cannot tell the difference between the initial signal and the great volume or intensity that has been added. At this point, the enemy's deception is complete, and we are unaware of the security breach. Being unaware, there is no alarm and no defensive action taken. As far as we are concerned, we took action on our own thoughts and feelings, unaware of the enemy's action. We don't recognize his contribution in magnifying, amplifying, or intensifying the initial thought or feeling, and he likes it that way. When we are unaware of the enemy's action, the tendency is to be less defensive, and, as such, we lose more battles. We must not regard any negative thoughts as insignificant. As a matter of fact, when these little thoughts are present, it is time to pray (war in the spirit), and even more so when these thoughts persist. There are times when the thoughts and desires we are wrestling with have such an enormous potential for pleasure and satisfaction that it becomes difficult for us to say it is wrong. But, if we have any doubt at all, this is a good time to ask God for help. There is nothing too difficult for God.

You must be vigilant when it comes to doing anything spiritual that will be beneficial to you; especially for the body of Christ in general, we will find all kinds of seemingly innocent, coincidental, distracting thoughts and ideas that will interrupt and discourage us from going forward. And despite what we know about the Word, these thoughts will try to exalt themselves above what it tells us about God. Without serious determination we will be mediocre and ineffective in our spiritual pursuits and objectives. If he—the enemy—cannot stop you from being a Christian, he will do his best to make you an impotent and ineffective one. The enemy will hide himself in many seemingly natural situations and do all kinds of spiritual damage. Don't be afraid to rebuke him when you recognize him. Jesus recognized him in Peter, in Matthew 16:23, "But He turned and said to Peter, 'Get behind me, Satan! You are an offense to Me, for you are not mindful of the things of God, but the things of men.'"(NKJV)

Notice Jesus did not address Peter; instead He said, "Get behind me, Satan!" Let us learn from the Master Himself. I don't believe that Peter was aware of the fact that he was under the influence of the devil; like Peter, you and I can be led astray as a loser in this spiritual war if we are unaware of the will and the Word of God. As Jesus continued to speak to Peter in verse 23, something fundamental becomes clear. Showing greater concern for the things of men rather than the things of God makes clear whose influence one is under. Based on the above scripture, the influence would be that of the enemy's; this is clearly offensive to God. When Jesus was faced with the choice between his life and a painful death, he chose death, which was the will of God. If we are in a war with the enemy, we cannot live according to the will of man, for man's will is often the will of the enemy. The occasion of Matthew 16:24-26 was not Peter's only experience with this type of temptation. He, unlike Jesus, was afraid of what man would say and/or do to him if he acknowledged being a friend of Jesus, in Matthew 26:69-75. As a result of fear, he denied Christ three times in one night, and this too was the work of the devil; according to the scripture (Luke 22:31), the devil was sifting him.

> *Then Jesus said to His disciples, "If anyone desires to come after Me, let him deny himself, and take up his cross, and follow Me. For whoever desires to save his life will lose it, but whoever loses his life for My sake will find it."*
>
> Matthew 16:24-25 (NKJV)

As children of God, we wrestle with enemies more powerful than us and more numerous than we can imagine. Without God on our side, we would have been destroyed long ago, but thank God for His mercy. Principalities, powers, and spiritual wickedness in high places are subject to Him, and His mercy protects us from the whims of the enemy. We must not forget who the real enemy is; he is not the person you are arguing with or thinking about in unfavorable ways. For the most part, what the enemy (the devil) is doing is not always obvious without the light of the Word of God. We may never see the devil with a gun or a knife, but we can see his violence in the actions of people with the guns and knives. We may never hear his voice directly, but when you hear and see violence, anger, or the venom of hatred, envy, pride, malice, lust, or bitterness, know for sure you are listening to the work of the devil. Don't expect him to come around with horns and a long tail with a fork in his hand. He will work for the most part the way he has always worked—undetected and behind the scenes.

We have examples to examine. Let us look at Judas. He may have had a weakness for money. He was the one in charge of the money among the disciples, and that may not be coincidental. 1 Timothy 6:10 (NKJV) says, *"the love of money is the root of all kind of evil,"* and the Devil knows how to exploit our weaknesses by way of his deceptions. He is the deceiver of individuals and nations.

> 3 *And Satan entered into Judas who was called Iscariot, belonging to the number of the twelve. 4 And he went away and discussed with the chief priests and officers how he might betray Him to them. 5 They were glad and agreed to give him money. 6 So he consented, and began seeking a good opportunity to betray Him to them apart from the crowd.*
>
> Luke 22:3-6 (NKJV)

There is nothing in the Word to indicate that Judas knew Satan had entered him. He was just like Peter, more concerned about the will of man rather than of the will of God. The impact of his action was not fully realized until the enemy's job was complete. By that time it was much too late. His entire attitude changed when he realized what he had done. We see that below in Matthew 27:3-5 (KJV):

> *Then Judas, which had betrayed Him, when he saw that he was condemned, repented himself, and brought again the thirty pieces of silver to the chief priests and elders, saying, "I have sinned in that I have betrayed the innocent blood." And they said, "What is that to us? See thou to that." And he cast down the pieces of silver in the temple, and departed, and went and hanged himself.*

Judas lost the battle through deception; he was an individual under the influence of the enemy. Deceiving the nations is the devil's job, and he is good at it, for so many have responded and continue to respond to his deception. The scriptures below show his influence on a large number of people and nations.

> *8 And shall go out to deceive the nations which are in the four quarters of the earth, Gog and Magog, to gather them together to battle: the number of whom is as the sand of the sea.*
>
> *9 And they went up on the breadth of the earth, and compassed the camp of the <u>saints</u> about, and the <u>beloved</u> city: and fire came down from God out of heaven, and devoured them.*
>
> Revelation 20:8-9 (KJV)
>
> *10 <u>And the devil that deceived them</u> was cast into the lake of fire and brimstone, where the beast and the false prophet are, and shall be tormented day and night forever and ever.*
>
> Revelation 20:10 (KJV)

The above prophetic Word has not yet taken place, but until that day he will continue to do his job as he has done in the past. When we look back through the pages of the Word, we can see what he did to Jesus, our Savior, through his age-old strategy of deception.

It is the realm of the demonic that brought about the death of Christ, although the enemy and his demons had no idea what they were doing.

In their ignorance, they unwittingly brought about the will of God. Jesus prayed to the Father regarding His death, "not my will but thine be done." It was the will of God that Jesus died to redeem man from death. The wisdom of God knows how to make even the enemy do His will. In our war against the enemy, the wisdom of God that is found in His Word is our ally, for it is a sword against the enemy.

1 Corinthians 2:7-8 (KJV) says

7 But we speak the wisdom of God in a mystery, even the hidden wisdom, which God ordained before the world unto our glory:

8 Which none of the princes of this world knew: for had they known it, they would not have crucified the Lord of glory.

Looking at the account of the crucifixion of Jesus Christ, we see many characters at work; human beings, such as Judas, Pilot, the high priest, Roman soldiers, and a large number of people shouting, "Crucify him." But the devil himself made no personal (natural) appearance. He was the puppet master, behind the scenes pulling the strings of his puppets that were ignorant enough to think that they were in control of their thoughts and actions. If the Word of God is true, they were clearly under deception. The enemy worked through the minds of all who were involved in the death of Christ. This is not man's opinion; it is the Word of God. Man without God is steeped in stupidity, as is the devil, who had no idea what he was doing when he caused the death of Christ, according to 1 Corinthians 2:8. Human wisdom begins with the fear of God without which we are far more vulnerable to the manipulation of the enemy. It is for this reason those responsible for His death were in the hands of the puppet master. They did not know and/or did not understand the Word of God. The devil made no personal appearance in that production, for he was off-screen, acting as writer, producer, and director. He can only be seen in the nature of his production. His mode of operation has not changed; on his stage, for the most part, he will not make personal appearances. But while we are being impressed with the performers and performances of his production, his seeds of deception and manipulation are being subliminally sewn deep in our subconscious mind. He does this by way of non-carnal principalities, powers, and spiritual wickedness in high places, supernaturally exerting deceptive influence upon our minds. Remember Ephesians 6:12:

> *For we do not wrestle against flesh and blood, but against principalities, against powers, against the rulers of the darkness of this age, and against spiritual hosts of wickedness in the heavenly places.*

Whom Are We Fighting?

Earlier we spoke about the fact that the weapons of our warfare are not flesh and blood nor natural, but spiritual. Now we must take a look at who or what our enemies are.

According to Ephesians 6:12, our enemies are not natural, but powerful, spiritual beings around us and in the heavenly realm above us. In the book of Daniel, we see the angel of God wrestling with one of these powerful spiritual beings. During this time in history, Syrus was the natural King of Persia. The demonic influence over this same area is referred to as the Prince of Persia. It is interesting to note that the angel that was fighting on behalf of Daniel won the battle with the help of Michael the archangel, according to Daniel 10:13. Not only do these spiritual beings try to influence the lives of individuals, but they also exert great influence on large geographical areas, such as kingdoms, cities, and nations. In this case, the one with the responsibility over Persia is called the Prince of Persia. In the book of Revelation, we see the chief of demons being bound and locked away in the abyss, where he will not be able deceive the nations for a thousand years. Interestingly enough, although we are talking about the enemy's influence on large areas, he still takes great interest in certain individuals; only in this context he targets the individuals who have influence over a large number of people; for instance, heads of states. This is made very clear in the book of Ezekiel, chapter 28. In Revelation, the chief deceives the nations, but in Ezekiel the enemies' objective is the Prince of Tyre.

Here, God addresses both the flesh and blood authorities and the demonic influences of the city.

> *The word of the LORD came to me again, saying,*
>
> *2 "Son of man, say to the prince of Tyre, 'Thus says the Lord GOD: "Because your heart is lifted up, and you say, 'I am a god, I sit in the seat of gods, in the midst of the seas'; yet you are a man, and not a god, though you set your heart as the heart of a god.*
>
> *3 Behold, you are wiser than Daniel; there is no secret that can be hidden from you.*
>
> *4 With your wisdom and your understanding you have gained riches for yourself, and gathered gold and silver into your treasuries.*
>
> *5 By your great wisdom in trade you have increased your riches, and your heart is lifted up because of your riches."*
>
> *6 Therefore thus says the Lord GOD:*
>
> *"Because you have set your heart as the heart of a god,*
>
> *7 Behold, therefore, I will bring strangers against you, the most terrible of the nations; and they shall draw their swords against the beauty of your wisdom, and defile your splendor.*
>
> *8 They shall throw you down into the pit, and you shall die the death of the slain in the midst of the seas.*
>
> *9 Will you still say before him who slays you, 'I am a god'? But you shall be a man, and not a god, in the hand of him who slays you.*
>
> *10 You shall die the death of the uncircumcised by the hand of aliens; for I have spoken," says the Lord GOD.'"*
>
> Ezekiel 28:1-10 (NKJV)

As the Lord addresses the Prince of Tyre, it is made abundantly clear that He was speaking to a man, in the flesh, and not some spiritual being. This prince was rich and wise, but full of pride. He had all that he needed to seal his own destruction. What is even more interesting is the fact that the prince seemed to be emulating the chief of demons, one who was brought low because of the things he possessed. As the Lord addresses the prince, this is what he has to say in Ezekiel 28:5: "...*your heart is lifted up because of your riches.*" In our quest for righteousness and as we war in the spirit, we must be alert. Our abundance makes us vulnerable to pride, and the more we possess, the more vulnerable we tend to be. Remember, it does not have to be material things. It can be wisdom, beauty, education, and scores of other things we may possess. It is the enemy within (pride) which is so subtle that most people are unaware of its presence and suffer without knowing why. Hosea 4:6 says, "*My people are destroyed because of a lack of knowledge.*" There is absolutely nothing more spiritually corrosive, destructive, subtle, and deceptive than pride. In essence, it created the devil. There is no one else in the Word of God that has started as high and lofty as Lucifer (the light bearer) and that has fallen so low. All this is because of his pride. Now after addressing the Prince of Tyre, the Lord also addresses the King of Tyre. Both the king and the prince rule over the same area. The prince is a human being. The king, however, is in a different realm, as he is a demonic spirit. He represents spiritual wickedness in high places, literally. His objective is to steal, kill, and destroy. Tyre is his domain, and the prince is directly under the king's influence, so much so that the prince reflects the king's nature. In the time of Ezekiel's existence, Tyre must have been a significant city, for this king was the devil himself—the chief of all demons—and he does not work alone. The scripture below describes this king, and it leaves no doubt as to who he is.

11 Lamentation for the King of Tyre

Moreover the Word of the LORD came to me, saying,

12 "Son of man, take up a lamentation for the king of Tyre, and say to him, 'Thus says the Lord GOD:
"You were the seal of perfection,
Full of wisdom and perfect in beauty.

13 *You were in Eden, the garden of God;*
Every precious stone was your covering:
The sardius, topaz, and diamond,
Beryl, onyx, and jasper,
Sapphire, turquoise, and emerald with gold.
The workmanship of your timbrels and pipes
Was prepared for you on the day you were created.

14 *You were the anointed cherub who covers;*
I established you;
You were on the holy mountain of God;
You walked back and forth in the midst of fiery stones.

15 *You were perfect in your ways from the day you were created,*
Till iniquity was found in you.

16 *By the abundance of your trading*
You became filled with violence within,
And you sinned;
Therefore I cast you as a profane thing
Out of the mountain of God;
And I destroyed you, O covering cherub,
From the midst of the fiery stones.

17 *Your heart was lifted up because of your beauty;*
You corrupted your wisdom for the sake of your splendor;
I cast you to the ground,
I laid you before kings,
That they might gaze at you.

18 *You defiled your sanctuaries*
By the multitude of your iniquities,
By the iniquity of your trading;
Therefore I brought fire from your midst;
It devoured you,
And I turned you to ashes upon the earth
In the sight of all who saw you.

19 All who knew you among the peoples are astonished at you;
You have become a horror,
And shall be no more forever.'"

Ezekiel 28:11-19 (NKJV)

According to the description we see in this scripture, there is no doubt that the one being described is the devil himself. Verse 14 says that he is *"the anointed cherub that covereth,"* and God who is speaking said, *"I established you."* A cherub is certainly not a man, but an angel, and not an ordinary one. The plural for cherub is cherubim. They are so special to God that it seems they are always at His side. The ark of God in Old Testament times, which represented the presence of God, always had a cherub at each end of it. The scripture repeatedly refers to God as the God that dwells between the cherubim[1]. Take Psalm 80:1 (NIV), "Give ear, O shepherd of Israel, you who lead Joseph like a flock; you who dwell between the cherubim."

The devil was one of these special angels, who became full of pride, and God almighty, who hates the sin of pride, cast him out of heaven as a profane thing. The book of Isaiah says, *"How hast thou fallen from heaven, O Lucifer, son of the morning! How art thou cast down to the ground, which didst weaken the nations!"* (Isaiah 14:12) In Luke 10: 18, the Lord Jesus said, *"And I saw Satan fall like lightning from heaven."* So yes, the King of Tyrus is the Devil himself. He is in charge of all demonic activities. Not only does he have demons working for him, but thousands of people are enlisted in his army, working everywhere, including the church.

The Enemy's Work in Our Churches

In the church satan's minions are very active, visible, and try to appear holy; many of them have a powerful spiritual influence. Don't forget they are working for the Father of Lies and Master of Deception. Ask God very prayerfully to open your eyes and to deliver you from the deceptive works of the enemy. It is incredible how many unsuspecting Christians are under the influence of the devil's ministers in church. "For such men are false apostles, deceitful workmen, masquerading as apostles of

Christ. And no wonder, for Satan himself masquerades as an angel of light, 2 Corinthians 11:13-14 (NIV). False religion, the occult, witchcraft, etc., are usually masked as good, but they function under the influence of religious spirits. The average Christian can be deceived.

It is exciting to know that all demonic power will ultimately be destroyed by the power of God, but until that time comes, we, the people of God, will continue to fight. It is necessary for our survival, and we are confident of the victory of God over evil.

The Weapons of Our Warfare

We now know that, despite the fact that we are physical human beings, our daily battles are not physical. This we know because the Word of God says, *"though we walk in the flesh we do not war according to the flesh for the weapons of our warfare are not physical, but mighty through God to the pulling down of strongholds,"* (2 Corinthians 10:3-4). We also know who our enemies are and where major battles are fought. Now we need to know what our spiritual weapons are and how to use them to defeat all these powerful spiritual entities. Victory on our own impossible. Our only chance of victory rests on whether or not we use the God-given spiritual weapons that we have at our disposal. Let us look at a few.

The Weapon of Fasting and Prayer

The first weapon we will look at has two components—fasting and prayer. These two work in concert, and together they are extremely potent. Daniel employed this weapon in chapter 10, as we have seen, and obtained supernatural results. The angels of God are at God's command, for they are His messengers. The Lord responded to Daniel's prayer by sending a mighty angel with a message to him. This angel was so powerful, that even though the men with Daniel could not see him, they all trembled at his presence and ran to hide themselves. Overwhelmed, Daniel could not stand and fell on his face in weakness. The angel had what it takes to strengthen him with a touch. Despite all the power the angel possessed, the Prince of Persia held him up in a fight for twenty-one days, and he had to get help from one of God's mighty warriors, Michael the archangel. The demonic Prince of Persia was so upset about the message coming through to Daniel that the angel of God was confronted on his way back again. It is wonderful to know that Daniel was heard on the first day; obviously, the enemy could not stop his prayer from going up to the Father. And though this demonic prince was so powerful, he could not stop Daniel from fasting and praying. Thank God he never had to deal directly with this powerful demonic spirit; he was protected as we are. Daniel's part in this mighty battle was prayer and fasting, and he won because the prince was defeated, for he could not stop the messenger and the message from coming to Daniel.

There are a few other weapons that we are going to examine. As we do so, we will find that many of these weapons overlap with one another. In fact, in most cases they must work in tandem with others, or they will not work at all. Obedience is one such weapon.

The Weapon of Obedience

The second weapon is obedience. Most Christians are familiar with the weapons of war, but are not using them correctly, and so they are ineffective. As a matter of fact, there are conditions when God will not even listen to His own people. In the scripture below we will see God rejecting prayer, sacrifice, worship, and praise from His own people because of a lack of obedience to His Word. Isaiah chapter 1: 10-20 (NIV) says,

> 10 Hear the Word of the LORD, you rulers of Sodom; listen to the law of our God, you people of Gomorrah!
>
> 11 "The multitude of your sacrifices--what are they to me?" says the LORD. "I have more than enough of burnt offerings, of rams and the fat of fattened animals; I have no pleasure in the blood of bulls and lambs and goats.
>
> 12 When you come to appear before me, who has asked this of you, this trampling of my courts?

13 Stop bringing meaningless offerings! Your incense is detestable to me. New Moons, Sabbaths and convocations—I cannot bear your evil assemblies.

14 Your New Moon festivals and your appointed feasts my soul hates. They have become a burden to me; I am weary of bearing them.

15 When you spread out your hands in prayer, I will hide my eyes from you; even if you offer many prayers, I will not listen. Your hands are full of blood;

16 wash and make yourselves clean. Take your evil deeds out of my sight! Stop doing wrong,

17 learn to do right! Seek justice, encourage the oppressed. Defend the cause of the fatherless, plead the case of the widow."

18 "Come now, let us reason together," says the LORD. "Though your sins are like scarlet, they shall be as white as snow; though they are red as crimson, they shall be like wool.

19 If you are willing and obedient, you will eat the best from the land;

20 but if you resist and rebel, you will be devoured by the sword." For the mouth of the LORD has spoken.

The Lord has made it clear that if we are not walking in obedience to His Word, He will not hear our prayers, neither will He pay any attention to our worship and praise; our offerings and sacrifices will be pointless, empty, and in vain. According to Isaiah 1:13, He says we must stop bringing meaningless offerings. This is what the Word says in 1 Chronicles 23:30-31: "And to stand every morning to thank and praise the LORD, and likewise at evening; and to offer all burnt sacrifices unto the LORD in the Sabbaths, in the new moon and on the set feasts, by number, according to the order commanded unto them continually before the LORD." Bear in mind, this is despite the fact that it was He who gave instructions to Israel about the new moon and Sabbath feast. Obviously, whatever God wants from His people is acceptable only on the condition of obedience, outside of which everything is meaningless to Him. Any powerful weapon mentioned will be rendered impotent without obedience. Verse 17 is a requirement for God to respond to us. We are required to do the right thing before God, such as to seek justice, to encourage the oppressed, to defend the cause of the fatherless, and to plead the cause of the widow. After we have applied verse 17, we will look at what God will do in verses 18 and 19; the God who would not listen to us will now reason with us, cleansing us of our sins and blessing us with the best of the land. The above scripture is by no means unique; there is great consistency in the Word of God.

The Bible does not negate itself. Essentially, if there appears to be any type of contradiction, it has to do with one or more scriptures taken out of context. There will always be direct or indirect references that will tie things together. As it relates to Isaiah 1, it connects very well to Isaiah 58. In a classic way, they confirm the essential message in each other, and it is far too vivid to miss. Let us see what Isaiah 58:1-3 has to say.

> *Cry aloud, spare not;*
> *Lift up your voice like a trumpet;*
> *Tell my people their transgression,*
> *And the house of Jacob their sins.*
>
> *2 Yet they seek me daily,*
> *And delight to know my ways,*
> *As a nation that did righteousness,*
> *And did not forsake the ordinance of their God.*
> *They ask of me the ordinances of justice;*
> *They take delight in approaching God.*
>
> *3 'Why have we fasted,' they say, 'and You have not seen?*
> *Why have we afflicted our souls, and You take no notice?'*

Isaiah 58:1-3 (NKJV)

In Isaiah 58, just as in chapter 1, we see the people of God doing very positive things. They were seeking God daily and taking delight in knowing His ways. They asked found of God the ordinances of justice and joy in approaching Him. Additionally, they were fasting and praying. If you and I were to randomly encounter people like these, we would probably assume that they are what God wants them to be. At a glance, they sure look like righteous people, but when we look at God's response, it becomes clear that they were only being religious. Being religious has a striking resemblance to Christianity. If we as the people of God are going to be victorious in our spiritual battles by employing the right weapons, we must be able to recognize the difference between being religious and walking in obedience to the Word of God. Genuine obedience involves more than the good things we traditionally do in church. It is clear that despite all of what was done in Isaiah 58:2–3—the fasting and praying, the desire to know His Word, the desire for judgment and justice, and even taking delight in knowing His ways—It was not enough to move God's hand. He would not respond to His own people for there was something missing. Matthew 7:21-23 (NKJV) says,

> Not everyone who says to Me, 'Lord, Lord,' shall enter the kingdom of heaven, but he who does the will of My Father in heaven. Many will say to Me in that day, 'Lord, Lord, have we not prophesied in Your name, cast out demons in Your name, and done many wonders in Your name?' And then I will declare to them, 'I never knew you; depart from Me, you who practice lawlessness!'

That "something missing" would be obedience. God wants us to do what He says, for when we do, it makes us strong against the enemy. If we aren't obedient, we will fall when the enemy comes against us. If we are not living in obedience, we will not be going anywhere; it is only a matter of time. Let's remember Matthew 7:24-27 (NKJV).[2] When we are disobedient to the Word of God we are being foolish, and foolishness cannot win battles. Our spiritual battles can only be won by the spirit and power of God, and without obedience, no victory is assured. Disobedience makes us unfruitful (John 15: 1-7), ineffective, impotent and prone to curses, according to Deuteronomy 28:15.

If we read all of Isaiah 58, we will see how beautifully God responds to obedience. As a sampling, let's look at verses 7-11 (NKJV) below:

7 *Is it not to share your bread with the hungry,*
And that you bring to your house the poor who are cast out;
When you see the naked, that you cover him,
And not hide yourself from your own flesh?

8 *Then your light shall break forth like the morning,*
Your healing shall spring forth speedily,
And your righteousness shall go before you;
The glory of the LORD shall be your rear guard.

9 *Then you shall call, and the LORD will answer;*
You shall cry, and He will say, 'Here I am.'
If you take away the yoke from your midst,
The pointing of the finger, and speaking wickedness,

10 *If you extend your soul to the hungry*
And satisfy the afflicted soul,
Then your light shall dawn in the darkness,
And your darkness shall be as the noonday.

11 *The LORD will guide you continually, and satisfy your soul in*
drought,
And strengthen your bones;
You shall be like a watered garden,
And like a spring of water, whose waters do not fail.

When we have done our part by walking in obedience to the Word of God, He will hear us.

Spiritual wars are fought on many fronts. The enemy is aware of this, and we must be as well. Yielding to the temptation to disobey His Word is one of these fronts.

The Weapon of Faith

The third weapon is faith. What is faith? According to Hebrews 11:1, "*Now faith is the substance of things hoped for, the evidence of things not seen.*" It is a very powerful weapon that must be employed. Without it we cannot please our God. Verse 6 says the following: "*but without faith it is impossible to please him, for he who comes to God must believe that he is, and that He is a rewarder of those who diligently seek him."* The enemy is absolutely no match for this non-carnal weapon of war; it is very powerful and creative. The entire universe was created by faith and the Word of God. The invisible God with invisible Word by invisible faith created all that is invisible as well as visible.

> *By faith we understand that the worlds were framed by the Word of God, so that the things which are seen were not made of things which are visible.*
>
> Hebrews 11:3 (NKJV)

The Lord wants us to know our true potential when we walk in faith. We can cause impossible things to come into being, and there is nothing the enemy can do to stop the impact of this weapon. The antithesis of faith, however, is unbelief, and it is the enemy's weapon against us. If we embrace unbelief, we will not see much of God's miracles. Matthew 13:58 says, *"But Jesus did not do many mighty works there because of their unbelief."* Unbelief is a thought that exalts itself against our faith, but we must bring it into captivity to the obedience of Christ. The knowledge of God is in His Word (Christ); His Word encourages us to have faith.

> *So Jesus said to them, "Because of your unbelief; for assuredly, I say to you, if you have faith as a mustard seed, you will say to this mountain, 'Move from here to there,' and it will move; and nothing will be impossible for you However, this kind does not go out except by prayer and fasting."*
>
> Matthew 17:20-21 (NKJV)

When we lack faith, we limit our experience with miracles and displease our God. Many people want to see the answer to prayers before they have faith, but it cannot work that way. We must believe we have already gotten what we have prayed for, before we see the answer to our prayer.

Therefore I say to you, whatever things you ask when you pray, believe that you receive them, and you will have them.

Mark 11:24 (NKJV)

The Weapon of Praise and Worship

The fourth weapon has two components—praise and worship. For the most part, these two usually work together. Let us begin with praise. Praise is absolutely necessary and essential in the life of a child of God. In fact, the Word of God says in Psalm 150:6, "*Let everything that has breath praise the Lord.*" God has done far more for us than we can praise Him for in our lifetime. And with all that He has done for us, praises should be as natural as the air we breathe. We are encouraged in the Word to offer the sacrifice of praise, which is the fruit of our lips. Sacrifice, in the context of an offering to God, speaks of an offering that comes by way of blood-shed, pain, and death. That is the kind of verbal praise we give to God when we have no natural desire to do so. On these occasions we are more comfortable being silent, but instead we put our natural desire to death, in order that the praises to God can come alive on our lips, although we don't feel like it. Praise involves the expression of gratitude, appreciation, and adoration of our God for all that He has done and will do for us. Praise to God is more than verbal expression. In Leviticus 19:23–24, we see God giving instruction to the children of Israel to offer the fruit of the land on the fourth year, as praise to Him.

When you come into the land, and have planted all kinds of trees for food, then you shall count their fruit as uncircumcised. Three years it shall be as uncircumcised to you. It shall not be eaten. But in the fourth year all its fruit shall be holy, a praise to the LORD.

Leviticus 19:23-25 (NKJV)

Praise includes dancing and the playing of musical instruments of all sorts. We see this in the Old Testament.

3 Let them praise His name with the dance;
Let them sing praises to Him with the timbrel and harp.

4 For the LORD takes pleasure in His people;
He will beautify the humble with salvation.

5 Let the saints be joyful in glory;
Let them sing aloud on their beds.

6 Let the high praises of God be in their mouth,
And a two-edged sword in their hand.

Psalm 149:3-6 (NKJV)

Beyond the fact that we should naturally want to praise God for His goodness and mercy towards us, the fringe benefits of praise are enormous. One major benefit is the privilege of experiencing the pleasure of the presence of the almighty God of the universe. With His presence comes the anointing, and with the anointing, yokes are broken.

There is no experience that can parallel feeling the presence of God Almighty. It is unspeakable and glorious beyond measure. Every human being should have this intimate, supernatural experience at least once. It is unforgettably addictive—once is never enough. Maybe those who have been addicted to drugs could relate to the feeling, in a sense. It is a shame that there are some Christians who have never experienced the manifested presence of God. The experience gives new meaning to the scriptures, Psalms 11:16, *"in his presence there is FULLNESS OF JOY; and at his right hand PLEASURES for evermore,"* and 1 Chronicles 16:27 that says, *"GLORY and HONOR are in his presence; STRENGTH and GLADNESS are in his place."*

It is often said that when we pray, our prayers go up to God through Jesus, but when we worship, His presence comes down to us. Psalms 22:3 says the following: *"but thou art holy. O thou that inhabits the praise of Israel."* The word from the Hebrew language that translates into "inhabits" is "yashab." It has several meanings. Let us look at a few, and you can make your choice as to which one you would prefer to use.

"Yashab" means "to sit down, to dwell, to remain, to settle." In other words, the Lord sits down, dwells, remains, or settles in the praise of

Israel. Now, we are not physical Israel, but we are spiritual Israel, according to the Word of God. In short, Israel is the seed of Abraham. *"Know ye therefore that they which are of faith, the same are the children of Abraham,"* (Galatians 3:7). And Romans 2:28, in the KJV, says, *"but he is a Jew who is one inwardly; and circumcision is that of the heart in the spirit and not in the letter."* The above explanation is necessary for us to understand that when we, the children of God, pour our hearts out in praise to our God, His presence will come to us because we are His people. Not only does His presence bring great pleasure, but it does massive damage to the realm of darkness. It is one of our most POWERFUL WEAPONS, as we war in the realm of the spirit. His presence is one of the benefits of praise. Worship and praise should be a significant part of our lifestyle and, as such, a daily experience for us.

The Two Dimensions of Worship

There are certain fundamental aspects of worship that we must understand in order to be effective. Worship has at least two distinct dimensions or phases; number one is the natural, and number two, the spiritual. The natural has to do with our initial approach to worship, which is intellectual. From the intellectual perspective, we think about all the good things that God offers us—such as His mercy, His grace, His provision, His protection, and so on. We praise His name with all our hearts, souls, and minds. All this, despite how genuinely involved and sincere we may be, is only entry-level worship. As long as our hands are clean, our hearts are pure, and we do not regard iniquity in our hearts, the Lord will hear us.

Don't Stop at Phase One

On the other hand, however, if we do not experience His quickening, His anointing, or His manifested presence, we are still in phase one of worship. It behooves us to continue pressing into His presence at phase one, until we experience His presence. No one will have to tell you when this occurs; you will know it and know it with all your heart. It is at this point that phase two of your worship begins. At this point, it becomes an irresistible pleasure that demands indulgence on a deep, spiritual level far beyond the intellectual entry point. God truly inhabits the praises of His people, and His presence is unmistakable. It is a common thing at this level of worship to see the gifts of the spirit in operation, and many people will discover what their spiritual gifts are for the first time. This supernatural phase of worship is where many people will experience the baptism of the Holy Ghost. Healing and deliverance take place, yokes and bondages are broken, and all the gifts of the spirit tend to be operational during this phase-two worship. Even as God is blessing us with His presence during worship, He is also causing immense damage in the kingdom of darkness on our behalf. We should note the fact that the more we give to God in terms of our sacrifice of praise, the greater His response to us will be. His Word says the same measure with which we give will be given back to us, according to Luke 6:38. We cannot out give God. Solomon was aware of God's response to praise when he dedicated the temple of God; he offered animal sacrifices in such large numbers that they lost count. 2 Chronicles 5:6 (NKJV) says, "Also King Solomon, and all the congregation of Israel who were assembled with him before the ark, were sacrificing sheep and oxen that could not be counted or numbered for multitude."

Along with the animal sacrifices, they lifted up their voices together with musical instruments and praised the name of the LORD in unison. To this great sacrifice God had a great response. His manifested presence was so vivid and powerful that the priest could not stand to minister in the temple. Some believe that they literally could not stand up in His manifested presence, so they all fell down.

2 Chronicles 5:11-14 (NKJV) says,

> 11 And it came to pass when the priests came out of the Most Holy Place (for all the priests who were present had sanctified themselves, without keeping to their divisions), 12 and the Levites who were the singers, all those of Asaph and Heman and Jeduthun, with their sons and their brethren, stood at the east end of the altar, clothed in white linen, having cymbals, stringed instruments and harps, and with them one hundred and twenty priests sounding with trumpets

13 indeed it came to pass, when the trumpeters and singers were as one, to make one sound to be heard in praising and thanking the LORD, and when they lifted up their voice with the trumpets and cymbals and instruments of music, and praised the LORD, saying: "For He is good,
For His mercy endures forever,"
that the house, the house of the LORD, was filled with a cloud, 14 so that the priests could not continue ministering because of the cloud; for the glory of the LORD filled the house of God.

The greatest sacrifice and praise recorded in the bible, brought about the greatest manifestation of the presence of God. As it relates to worship working as a weapon against the enemy, 2 Chronicles 20 could not make this point any clearer. In a nutshell, a number of armies came against Israel to war. They far outnumbered Israel. The king's response to the threat was fear, so he went to God for help. In 2 Chronicles 20:3 (KJV) we read about him confessing to God that they had no power against such a vast army. It says, "And Jehoshaphat feared, and set himself to seek the LORD, and proclaimed a fast throughout all Judah."

In 2 Chronicles 20:12:

O our God, wilt thou not judge them? For we have no might against this great company that cometh against us; neither know we what to do: but our eyes are upon thee.

The Lord advised the king to put the marching band ahead of the army to sing praises to God. They did as the Lord had told them; they went to war singing praises to God and won a great victory. The Lord brought confusion within the enemy's army, so much so that they fought against themselves and destroyed each other.

2 Chronicles 20:21-22 (KJV) says,

21 And when he had consulted with the people, he appointed singers unto the LORD, and that should praise the beauty of holiness, as they went out before the army, and to say, "Praise the LORD; for his mercy endureth forever."

22 And when they began to sing and to praise, the LORD set ambushments against the children of Ammon, Moab, and mount Seir, which were come against Judah; and they were smitten.

Praise is multifaceted; we give God what is due to Him. Praise causes us to experience the presence and the blessings of God. Praise is also a WEAPON, for it will bring many victories in the realm of the spirit, and it destroys the Kingdom of Darkness. It is not carnal, but mighty through God to the pulling down of strongholds.

Despite the fact that so many of us are unaware, spiritual wars in which many battles are fought on a daily basis are a reality. This is by no means some new phenomenon. The fact is spiritual wars are older than the human race. They began in heaven, when the devil rebelled against his maker and was cast out by the angels of God.

7 And there was war in heaven: Michael and his angels fought against the dragon; and the dragon fought and his angels,

8 And prevailed not; neither was their place found any more in heaven.

9 And the great dragon was cast out, that old serpent, called the Devil, and Satan, which deceiveth the whole world: he was cast out into the earth, and his angels were cast out with him.

Revelation 12:7-9 (KJV)

Notice where the devil came after he was cast out of heaven—right here in the earthly realm where man exists. And not long after our arrival we were engaged in our first spiritual battle. We lost, and the impact was deadly. Death came to the human race. Every funeral is a reminder of the effect of sin. And every time we smell the stench of decaying road kill it is a reminder of the effect of sin until this day. It is not enough for the enemy that death passes upon all man. We, by virtue of being the object of the Father's love, incur the wrath of the enemy; he has been relentless in his effort to destroy us ever since. He works in the darkness of the invisible realm of the spirit, but his impact is manifested in the natural, as in the case of physical death. The devil is a spirit being, who by way of temptation from the realm of the spirit impacted the lives of Adam and Eve in the realm of the natural. The impact affected them both in the natural and the spiritual, in that spiritual death occurred instantly the moment they touched and ate the forbidden fruit. Physical death, however, was a process. It began at the same moment, but it finished over 900 years later. "And all the days that Adam lived were nine hundred and thirty years: and he died," Genesis 5:5 (KJV).

Made In His Image

We humans are made in the image of God, so we are spirit beings, but we are veiled in flesh. As a result, we don't readily see beyond the veil (flesh) into the realm of the spirit. The Devil is aware of our inability to naturally see in this area without knowledge of and obedience to the Word of God, so he has been taking full advantage of us from the time we entered the Garden of Eden until now. Seeing through this veil that obscures our vision requires the Word of God, for His Word is our light and our lamp. "Thy word is a lamp unto my feet, and a light unto my path." Psalm 119:105 (KJV). The almighty God by way of His Word has given great insight into the realm of the spirit. When our Lord Jesus Christ died on Calvary, the veil of the temple was rent in two, signifying that we, the children of God, no longer needed the earthly priest to go into the presence of God for us. *"19 Having therefore, brethren, boldness to enter into the holiest by the blood of Jesus, 20 By a new and living way, which he hath consecrated for us, through the veil, that is to say, his flesh,"* KJV. The word veil means covering, such as a curtain. It also means flesh, such as what we are covered in, and this is no coincidence. The veil, which stood between sinful man and a holy God in the temple, seems to symbolize the flesh, and, apart from the high priest, no sinful flesh could enter into the holy presence of God. But Jesus Christ, who had no sin, made a sacrifice of Himself for us, and by His shed blood

He consecrated and dedicated a pathway, by which we can enter into the presence of God. When the flesh of Jesus Christ was torn so was the symbol of flesh in the temple: the veil of the temple was rent in two, and now we can go through the torn flesh (veil) of Jesus into the holy of holies, into the very presence of the almighty God. Now we are members of the royal priesthood, and we can enter the holy place ourselves into the presence of God. Now, we cannot see this holy place, but we know we are there by faith because the Word of God (our lamp and our light) says so. Notice that the veil is not removed, but there is a path through which we can go—Jesus Christ himself. *"Jesus answered, 'I am the way and the truth and the life. No one comes to the Father except through me,'* John14:6 (NIV). By the same token, we know that we are wrestling principalities and powers and spiritual wickedness in high places. We also know that we are not using natural, but spiritual weapons in our fight, because the Word says so. We cannot see the holy place or the pathway through the veil by which we enter God's presence. We know we enter His presence because of the light of His Word. Without the Word of God we would be walking in darkness, but there is no need to. God grants us the wisdom to use the light (the Word of God). In the book of Chronicles, David and the children of Israel suffered tremendously at the hand of the enemy working from behind the veil. David was defeated in this spiritual battle with Satan. He won many natural battles with the help of the spirit of God, but when his pride got in the way it was an open door for the enemy, and so he came under the influence of the Devil who defeated him. 1 Chronicles 21:1 (KJV), "And Satan stood up against Israel, and provoked David to number Israel."

> *14 So the Lord sent pestilence upon Israel: and there fell of Israel seventy thousand men.*
>
> *15 And God sent an angel unto Jerusalem to destroy it: and as he was destroying, the Lord beheld, and he repented him of the evil, and said to the angel that destroyed, "It is enough, stay now thine hand."*
>
> 2 Samuel? 24:14-15 (KJV)

We cannot afford to lose our battles, they are too costly. We must be alert and stay in a state of awareness to the fact that we are spiritual beings, and our temptations are generated by a spiritual enemy, such as the one that came against David. It is for this reason we are reminded that we don't wrestle with flesh and blood, and our weapons of war are not fleshly. Yes, we have been in a war from the time we were placed on earth, and the enemy is still the same spiritual being.

Walk Into the Light

When we allow the Devil to have his way and win the battles in which we are engaged, we incur the Judgment of God upon our lives. Despite the fact that the Devil is ultimately responsible for sin, it does not absolve us from guilt when we yield to his temptation. The enemy may be trying to take us in one direction, but the Word of God is rich with instruction for us. In short, we are expected to resist the enemy and walk into the light. Ultimately, we must make the decision between light and darkness, whether we want to walk in the flesh or in the spirit. If we allow the gratification of our own emotions and desires to take precedence over the Word of God, then we are walking in darkness and in the flesh which is the will of the enemy, for he promotes fleshly desires. It is unfortunate that our tendency is to please the flesh.

> *19 This is the verdict: Light has come into the world, but men loved darkness instead of light because their deeds were evil.*
>
> *20 Everyone who does evil hates the light, and will not come into the light for fear that his deeds will be exposed.*
>
> *21 But whoever lives by the truth comes into the light, so that it may be seen plainly that what he has done has been done through God.*
>
> John 3:19-22

We cannot experience victory in this war without living and walking in the spirit.

This I say then, "Walk in the Spirit, and ye shall not fulfill the lust of the flesh."

Galatians 5:16 (KJV)

Fulfilling the lust of the flesh is losing a battle in the war.

If we live in the Spirit, let us also walk in the Spirit.

Galatians 5:25

How do we walk in the spirit? We walk in the spirit when we do what the Word of God says.

63 It is the spirit that quickeneth; the flesh profiteth nothing: the words that I speak unto you, they are spirit, and they are life.

John 6:63 (KJV)

20 My son, attend to my words; incline thine ear unto my sayings.

21 Let them not depart from thine eyes; keep them in the midst of thine heart.

22 For they are life unto those that find them, and health to all their flesh.

Proverbs 4:20-22 (KJV)

God Is Our Father

God is our father, and He is the Word. "In the beginning was the word and the word was with God and the word was God." John 1:1 He loves us so much that He put on flesh and became a human being, in order to redeem us from the impact of the first battle that we lost in the Garden of Eden.

> *The Word of God became flesh and made his dwelling among us. We have seen his glory, the glory of the One and Only, who came from the Father, full of grace and truth.*

> John 1:14 (NIV)

God expresses Himself through His Word (Jesus Christ).

> *In the past God spoke to our forefathers through the prophets at many times and in various ways, but in these last days he has spoken to us by his Son, whom he appointed heir of all things, and through whom he made the universe.*

> Hebrews 1:1-2 (NIV)

Jesus Christ is the personification of the Word of God, which is God. (John 1:1)

It is for this reason Jesus is referred to as the Word of God in the book of Revelations.

> *He was clothed with a robe dipped in blood, and His name is called the Word of God.*

> Revelations 19:13 (NKJV)

His robe dipped in blood speaks of His crucifixion, and those of us who receive the crucified Christ (the Word of God) are empowered to become sons of God. But as many as received Him, to them He gave power to become the sons of God, even to them that believe in His name:

> *13 which were born, not of blood, nor of the will of the flesh, nor of the will of man, but of God.*

> John 1:12-13 (KJV)

Redeemed From Spiritual Death

> *"The virgin will be with child and will give birth to a son, and they will call him Immanuel"—which means, "God with us."*

> Matthew 1:22-23 (NIV)

God literally came among us and fought on our behalf. He took our sin that we may walk in His victory. As born-again children of God this is our first victory.

> *For he hath made him to be sin for us, who knew no sin; that we might be made the righteousness of God in him.*

> 2 Corinthians 5:21 (KJV)

Jesus Christ is the image of the Father.

> *13 For he has rescued us from the dominion of darkness and brought us into the kingdom of the Son he loves, 14 in whom we have redemption,*

the forgiveness of sins. He is the image of the invisible God, the firstborn over all creation.

Colossians 1:13-15 (NIV)

When we apply the Word of God to our lives, it transforms us into the image of His son. Romans 8:29 (NKJV) reads,

For whom He foreknew, He also predestined to be conformed to the image of His Son, that He might be the firstborn among many brethren.

Becoming a son of God is my greatest victory over the enemy, and there are more victories to come. God being my Father positioned me for victory, for I have the greatest power of the universe on my side; if I do what He requires of me, He promises to respond to my request. And when He does, there can only be one outcome, for God cannot fail.

If ye abide in me, and my words abide in you, ye shall ask what ye will, and it shall be done unto you.

1 John 15:7 (KJV)

God is Light and so is His Word/Son

"This then is the message which we have heard of him, and declare unto you, that <u>God is light, and in him is no darkness at all</u>"

1 John 1:5 (KJV)

Who only hath immortality, <u>dwelling in the light which no man can approach unto</u>; whom no man hath seen, nor can see: to whom be honor and power everlasting. Amen.

1 Timothy 6:16 (KJV)

As it relates to the Son, it is no surprise that He shares the same attributes and duties with the Father. He is also referred to as the light.

"Then spake Jesus again unto them, saying, "I am the light of the world: he that followeth me shall not walk in darkness, but shall have the light of life."

John 8:12 (KJV)

Below are three examples of the common attributes/titles they share, as they are both one and the same. 1) KING, 2) JUDGE, and 3) CREATOR/MAKER.

Statement about God (Yehovah/Jehovah)

For the Lord is our judge, the Lord is our lawgiver, the Lord is our king; he will save us.

Isaiah 33:22 (KJV)

Statement about Jesus

Then said the chief priests of the Jews to Pilate, Write not, The <u>King</u> of the Jews; but that he said, I am King of the Jews.

John 19:21 (KJV)

Statement about God (Elohiym)

And the heavens shall declare his righteousness: for God is <u>judge</u> himself. Selah.

Psalm 50:6 (KJV)

Statement about Jesus

I charge thee therefore before God, and the Lord Jesus Christ, who shall <u>judge</u> the quick and the dead at his appearing and his kingdom.

2 Timothy 4:1 (KJV)

Statement by the Lord (Yahweh/Jehovah)

Thus saith the Lord, thy redeemer, and he that formed thee from the womb, I am the Lord <u>that maketh all things; that stretcheth forth the heavens alone; that spreadeth abroad the earth by myself</u>.

Isaiah 44:24 (KJV)

Statement about Jesus

In whom we have redemption through his blood, even the forgiveness of sins:

15 Who is the image of the invisible God, the firstborn of every creature.

16 For by him were all things created, that are in heaven, and that are in earth , visible and invisible, whether they be thrones, or dominions, or principalities, or powers: all things were created by him, and for him:

Colossians 1:14-16 (KJV)

The impact of our obedience to the Word of God is far reaching and multifaceted. Not only do we know by faith in the Word of God that we are sons/daughters of the Most High, but we also become light as we walk in the light of His Word, reflecting the nature of the father and the son.

For ye were sometimes darkness, but now are ye light in the Lord: walk as children of light.

Ephesians 5:8 (KJV)

Ye are the light of the world. A city that is set on an hill cannot be hid.

Matthew 5:14 (KJV)

As children of the light (God), we walk in His authority and power of God (light), and demonic spirits and powers are subject to us according to the Word of God. Casting out demons is another way we battle in the realm of the spirit, just like Jesus did. And He has instructed us to do as He did.

> *And these signs shall follow them that believe; in my name shall they cast out devils; they shall speak with new tongues.*
>
> Mark 16:17 (KJV)

> *Heal the sick, cleanse the lepers, raise the dead, cast out devils: freely ye have received, freely give.*
>
> Matthew 10:8 (KJV)

> *17 A man in the crowd answered, "Teacher, I brought you my son, who is possessed by a spirit that has robbed him of speech.*
>
> *18 Whenever it seizes him, it throws him to the ground. He foams at the mouth, gnashes his teeth and becomes rigid. I asked your disciples to drive out the spirit, but they could not."*
>
> *19 "O unbelieving generation," Jesus replied, "how long shall I stay with you? How long shall I put up with you? Bring the boy to me."*
>
> *20 So they brought him. When the spirit saw Jesus, it immediately threw the boy into a convulsion. He fell to the ground and rolled around, foaming at the mouth.*
>
> *21 Jesus asked the boy's father, "How long has he been like this?" "From childhood," he answered.*
>
> *22 "It has often thrown him into fire or water to kill him. But if you can do anything, take pity on us and help us."*
>
> *23 "'If you can'?" said Jesus. "Everything is possible for him who believes."*

24 Immediately the boy's father exclaimed, "I do believe; help me overcome my unbelief!"

25 When Jesus saw that a crowd was running to the scene, he rebuked the evil spirit. "You deaf and mute spirit," he said, "I command you, come out of him and never enter him again."

Mark 9:17-25 (NIV)

Spiritual battles are fought in more than one arena; sometimes it has to do with the control of our thoughts, and sometimes it has to do with the spoken word. God, our Father, has taught us how to achieve victory by His Word. May God grant us the courage to walk in His Word and win our battles.

Some other scriptures regarding pride—Proverbs 16:18 and 29:23, James 4:6

[1] See Psalm 99:4, Isaiah 37:16, and 2 Kings 19:15

[2] "Therefore whoever hears these sayings of Mine, and does them, I will liken him to a wise man who built his house on the rock: 25 and the rain descended, the floods came, and the winds blew and beat on that house; and it did not fall, for it was founded on the rock. 26 But everyone who hears these sayings of Mine, and does not do them, will be like a foolish man who built his house on the sand: 27 and the rain descended, the floods came, and the winds blew and beat on that house; and it fell. And great was its fall." (NKJV)

LaVergne, TN USA
24 August 2010
194450LV00002B/1/P